urban creatures – robert martens

*Then they said,
"Come, let us build ourselves a city,
with a tower that reaches to the heavens,
so that we may make a name for ourselves;
otherwise we will be scattered over
the face of the whole earth."*

(Genesis 11:4)

also by robert martens

finding home (silver bow publishing) 2022
city of beasts (ekstasis editions) 2019
hush (ekstasis editions) 2016
little creatures (ekstasis editions) 2013

urban creatures

by Robert Martens

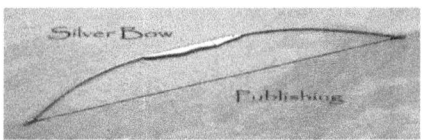

Silver Bow Publishing
720 Sixth Street, Box # 5
New Westminster, BC
CANADA   V3L3C5

Title: urban creatures
Author: Robert Martens
Cover Art: "Critter" painting by Candice James
Cover Design: Candice James
Layout and Editing: Candice James
ISBN: 9781774033814(print)
ISBN: 9781774033821 (e-book)

All rights reserved including the right to reproduce or translate this book or any portions thereof, in any form except for the use of short passages for review purposes, no part of this book may be reproduced, in part or in whole, or transmitted in any form or by any means, electronically or mechanically, including photocopying, recording, or any information or storage retrieval system without prior permission in writing from the publisher or a license from the Canadian Copyright Collective Agency (Access Copyright)

ISBN: 9781774033814 (print)
ISBN: 9781774033821 (ebook)
© Silver Bow Publishing 2025

Library and Archives Canada Cataloguing in Publication Title: Urban creatures / by Robert Martens. Other titles: Urban creatures (Compilation) Names: Martens, Robert, 1949- author. Description: Includes bibliographical references. Identifiers: Canadiana (print) 20250255413 | Canadiana (ebook) 20250259117 | ISBN 9781774033814 (softcover) | ISBN 9781774033821 (Kindle) Subjects: LCGFT: Poetry. Classification: LCC PS8626.A7687 U73 2025 | DDC C811/.6—dc23

urban creatures – robert martens

**Dedicated to my parents
and grandparents
who raised me with love.**

Go on, builders in hope :
tho' Jerusalem wanders far away,
Without the gate of Los:
among the dark Satanic wheels.

- William Blake

I dream'd in a dream I saw a city
invincible to the attacks
of the whole of the rest of the earth,
I dream'd that was the new city of Friends,
Nothing was greater there
than the quality of robust love,
it led the rest,
It was seen every hour
in the actions of the men of that city,
And in all their looks and words.

- Walt Whitman

Praise for "urban creatures"

Abbotsford's modern-day beat poet, Robert J. Martens, has produced another provocative volume of poems. How to sum it up? These lines do so: "based (loosely, as in the movies) on a true story." "we are refugees from the womb that bore us." "he's stumbling towards/assembly." Time, mentioned fifty times, and home, thirty-one, are the undertow. As with the beat poets of the '50s, Martens' poems are in free verse, often surrealistic, told in the cadence of his "mennonite half-glass" past, hymns, and snippets of conversations he's had with people in bars, street corners, and while travelling abroad. The mix of moody, playful, mischievous, and humorous poems beg to be read "slow as a snail/ on a salty day." ~**Elsie K Neufeld personal historian, poet, and essayist.**

A poet's take on the homelessness of displacement, of cultural security gone missing, in a way that holds the reader like a thriller novel. "Tinged with divinity," poems flow in vulnerable revelation through the hope and reality of immigration with paradoxes like "the sun being ice," a timely call to direct the course of our borders and intentions to global grace. From "the eons that birthed us" to "rusted cans/ looking at the stars" "where/ quarks can be named only/ as music. as prayer," Martens addresses the complexity of the deep-rooted desire to belong. In detailed physics he expands deeply into zen, grappling with the mysteries and science of the universe, then lands readers back in the elegant truth that "there/ is a point, we can/ step into the day...feed and clothe/ the least of these,/ we can love/ minute by minute." Advocating for genuine compassion rather than bowing to left or right icons, Martens affirms that how we treat and make space for each other is paramount to securing a humane world for all – we are all in need of absolution. ~**Cynthia Sharp, Canada's Mary Oliver, Award-winning Author of** *Ordinary Light & Rainforest in Russet*

Robert Martens' poetry is urgent and intimate – deeply human, richly emotive, and achingly expressive. These extraordinary poems will not only draw you in, but quietly transform you. He writes into the heart of complexity: identity, deprivation, ecology, aging, harmony – each theme delicately woven, each word carrying weight. This is a collection shaped by narrative soul, lyrical vision, and the quiet undercurrents of the mind. Through these poems, Robert shows us how life appears through his eyes – and how it feels in his bones. His language is a gentle touch, a soft knock at the door, a whisper carried on the wind. It holds the quiet, steady power to heal, to awaken, to reshape the lives and worlds it enters. ~**Ashok Bhargava, President Writers International Network, BC.**

Contents

exiles in the city / 11

borders / 13
petrus / 17
one hundred (thousand) years later / 19
stalin's poet / 20
philosophy 101 with a gospel minor / 21
down to the river to pray / 22

the city at zero / 23

cheap beer and laptops . 25
prayer #9 (after ezra pound / 26
green grief / 27
against the red / 28
middle class / 29
bad animation / 30
ecology / 31
where home / 32
fixers / 33
pale rider / 35

sunday morning in the suburbs / 37

sunday morning / 39

citylab whitecoats / 47

playing dice with the universe / 49
there will be (no) blood / 52
space / 53

e=mc²/ / 54
ctrl-alt-delete / 55

red lights and cellphone streets / 57

diagnosis / 59
it came upon a midnight clear / 60
call me when you have time / 61
prayer #8 (after jeff tweedy) / 62
prayer #7 (after jeff tweedy) / 63
prayer #6 (after jeff tweedy) / 64
prayer #5 (after jeff tweedy) / 65
prayer #1 (after jeff tweedy) / 66
prayer #2 (after jeff tweedy) / 67
pickup truckers hauling ass / 68
and my cellphone kept talking / 69
elegy for a pop star / 70

urban creatures / 71

urban creatures / 73-82

urban legends / 83

based (loosely, as in the movies) on a true story / 85
white nights / 87
missing / 88
unprotected borders / 90
shoeshine / 91
cruising to byzantium / 92

call now! retire in the city / 97

the mystery of our aging / 99

comedy club, cash bar only / 107

can one, let me see, how do i phrase this... / 109
not the minutes / 110
the drunkard's farewell / 111
the red dogs bark at midnight / 113
buddha and the guys / 114
the community of saints / 116
a nostalgic look back / 118

four-part harmony on golden streets / 121

pandemic in the suburbs / 123
then and now and then / 124
in every grain of sand / 125
resurrection between the lines / 126
noise data / 127
coffee cantata / 128
average / 129
mistakes / 130
the highs and lows / 131
winter solstice / 132
anger / 134
household spirit / 137
sometimes / 138

author profile / 139

urban creatures – robert martens

exiles in the city

urban creatures – robert martens

borders

1

i dare you

and there it was, just beyond
our fingertips. we arrived
with documents, but would they
be enough?

the border guards were hulking
relics of the civil war.
i dare you, he said, *to
cross this line.*

we shuffled forward, hunched
in white winter coats, carrying
guidebooks to life in
the other world.

the sun was ice as we approached
the border. immigrants, or refugees,
i can't remember now, and
history books lie.

2.

what is the purpose

a bare light bulb,

a desk, papers,
a bureaucrat wearing glasses,
a muffled scream down the hallway.

the long line, waiting
outside, the tramp
of boots, passports
clutched in fingers numbed by wind.

home might be
behind us, at the end
of a loose gravel road,
might be a place yet unimagined.

name, number,
he said, bent
to his books, and
what is the purpose of your pointless journey?

3.

safety

in the new world, we
were daily strangers,
laboured to be like
the others.

each word we spoke
was foreign, we carried
work documents and
language cards.

each morning was an
experiment, new streets,
new cities bordering
our shelter.

each evening we
dreamed of home,
the safety of childhood
and custom.

4.

stories my mother told me

siberia was home, she said,
a good place to grow up,
my father always talked
about the big city, we
didn't want to leave,
life was good, our neighbours
thought we were mad
to go to canada, but we
sold the farm, made a
good profit, and in canada
my parents thought it was
a mistake. we were

dirt poor in the prairies,
but we didn't know it,
everyone, everyone was
the same, i wore a dress
my mother made from a flour sack,
and i watched over my brother
on the walk to school. one

day something was happening
in the corner of the
schoolyard, some boys
forced another boy to take off
his pants. for many years,

we wanted to go back
to siberia, to our home.

petrus

stories our father told us,
passed down to these
tame times. legends,
fables, myths. words
are hostage to memory.

petrus, our grandfather,
dreamer, schoolteacher,
believer, and in bolshevik
russia, these things
were criminal. they
came for him in their
ragged rage. they
stood him, said our father,
against the house, and
raised their rifles. in
that moment, those
precious seconds, how
dear this life, how
filled with voice and
snow and sleep and
endless skies. and

the love of a neighbour,
who pulled on a party
uniform, this one's alright,
he said, he's not rich,
he cares for the children.
rifles lowered. this
time, they said, this time.
then boots, curses, hoofbeats,
and they were gone.
silence. that same night

they abandoned their home,
fled to moscow,
found a new and
restless home overseas.

urban creatures – robert martens

all untrue, says the youngest
son. perhaps. but he
wasn't there, and in
these tame times,
this story of mercy,
dropped into our hands,
whispers from those before.

one hundred (thousand) years later

My forebears fled Ukraine
after the First and Second World Wars.

to maintain faith
in the breath of cold dawn

> *butchery in ukraine*
> *one century ago*

to taste consolation
in the silences between

> *and again, after the second*
> *great war, blood in the snow*

to hear voices
pleading final forgiveness

> *the same, again,*
> *murder unceasing*

to witness the end
of tanks and rubble

> *and again, and again*
> *we will not see the day*

to find mercy
in the icestorm of our souls

stalin's poet

Comrade Stalin, I was beside the sea on the Isla Negra,
resting from the struggle and the travels,
when the message about your death
came like a blow from the ocean.
  - Pablo Neruda, "Ode to Stalin"

the difference, said tolstoy, between
leftwing and rightwing tyranny

is the difference between
catshit and dogshit.

am i clear, pablo neruda,
your ghost circling my left brain,

and all the millions murdered
by your man stalin.

you accepted the peace prize
from his dripping hands.

hero of the left, pablo,
icon of the struggle,

did you write enough pretty words
to absolve your sins?

i could say this to your ghost, pablo,
no need for a poem,

couplets don't do justice,
and justice will never be.

let's kneel together, brother,
and pray for prosaic absolution.

philosophy 101 with a gospel minor

This world is not my home
I'm just a-passing through
My treasures are laid up
Somewhere beyond the blue
The angels beckon me
From heaven's open door
And I can't feel at home
In this world anymore

no axioms, no syllogisms,
in the lecture hall of my soul,
but questions thrown my way
by a professor who caught me asleep –

(1) i have always felt homeless, sir,
and hence have researched my history,
the genealogy, and the firing squads,
the famine, the riders at dawn,
the rifle butt pounding the door,
my refugee family with faith in their bags,
this world is not my home –

(2) i continue to feel homeless, sir,
and hence have driven the jigsaw streets,
through suburbs split by sonic walls,
through towers of tenants slumped on sofas,
and we have prospered, sir, and yet
we are refugees from the womb that bore us,
i'm just a-passing through –

(3) and yet, sir, a syllogism,
and perhaps, when class is dismissed, an axiom,
i was caught asleep, sir, and apologize,
i dreamed of a pathway through a valley,
of birdcall, wild scat, resurrected language,
poor philosophy, sir, but as the busker intones,
not my home, but one helluva walk –

down to the river to pray

childhood was only memory,
always memory. we peered back
through the willows at the riverbank,
through the receding mountain fog,
at the eons that birthed us.
we heard the confidence
in our voices that lengthened
days into years. our elders
were tinged with divinity.
secrets in the wind, the high grass.

then, the babble of towers.
cities scrambled as i slept.
the hours jittered
at the corners of my eyes,
quick as an oil yard flame.
stone shuddered and split. after
the sirens passed, my
voice was fevered. undeserved
peace. for an instant, for an
eon, always memory.

the city at zero

urban creatures – robert martens

cheap beer and laptops

overnight, the city has fallen.

warfare, or plague, or mere complacency,
whatever has transpired,
its end is complete.

flashing lights in the gutters.

coins in deadmen's pockets.

cracked tables, shattered wine bottles,
cellphones bent double, streets
of a useless empire, rusted cans
looking at the stars.

at sunrise, the dispossessed emerge.

they examine the blueprints.

they build a city replica, smaller,
of course, and wasted,
but it will endure.

until the empire sends its spies.

prayer #9 (after jeff tweedy+ezra pound)

the gods are returning,
says ezra of the milky eyes
to mussolini,
they're highstepping down
the freeway median,
swooping over
construction cranes,
there's a gilded swan
whispering in your ear,
a giant grinding a thunderbolt
in the bathroom,
and gentle ones too,
with oracles of kindness,
we betrayed them,
says ezra,
and we'll pay,
there will be blood,
this is a war
without end

green grief

as the city passes into smoke.

as we go about our day.

as beasts are driven from
    their ancient homes.

as another suburb squats.

green grief.

i have childhood memories
    of sky
    and fields
    and glacial rivers.

green grief. last night

the powers rubberstamped everything,
    it's a go.
    good, reasonable men and women.

but it's the lunatics with
    lava in their hearts,
    with broken words, who said,

we know we won't change anything,
    but we tried.

green knights.

as the city passes into smoke.

against the red

the homeless man on the crosswalk
has travelled from the other side
of the globe

he's lugging his pack of misery, and
his pace is slow as a snail
on a salty day

the crosswalk light is red, red
is my face, and my knuckles
white on the wheel

is that a multitude of horns,
or a chainsaw effect, or the zipper
in my skull

it's the day ripped open and
twenty-three hours to go,
curses at the crosswalk

the homeless man is shuffling to the other
side of the globe, he relies on
kindness and good brakes

he has nothing but time

middle class

we were born indifferent,
on the equinox at noon.

the time here is as calculated,
it plays like a nerdy game.

our cities merged as required,
and freeways to take us there.

we sit and drink our wine,
we friends who've never met.

a beggar at the next table,
words littered at our feet.

is there anything to say?
i have a sweet confession:

i was born indifferent,
but the time, the time has come –

we've learned no lesson but this:
as we rise and say goodbye.

bad animation

spine bent to earth,
forehead furrowed
by winds of time,
naked old man in the woods.

he's a caricature
of self, a cartoon
walking zombie,
brain cells dribbling on moss.

his bones crack,
he's a joke, he's
yourself on a bad day,
will the rain wake you from dream?

he's stumbling towards
assembly, and the lure
of knives in backs,
thorns tight in his knotted fist.

a call, a creature,
is it loneliness
to dementia?
but forgiveness in every leaf,

and mercy in
the vast opening
sky, in the black
soil that runs through his veins.

ecology

*floods, heat, flame, always
someone to blame, and is it
us, earth's children, earth's shame...*

I

fire and water,
hoofbeats, raise
the guard, man
empire's walls,
cry the imminent
invasion.

II

fire and water,
silence, scouts,
the invisible enemy,
we entered the
court, the empire is
us.

III

fire and water,
freeways, suburbs,
speed, revenge is
hers, she'll take us
back, oceans,
suns.

where home

the mountain slashed
and levelled for human
comfort. our concrete
valley. the green
receding, diminishing daily,
deer fleeing to
distant hills,
birdsong quieter
with each dawning.

and the hungry haul
of traffic, our city
growing obese as she
swallows life and
limb. but the crows,

crafty creatures,

we watching them
at nightfall,
their silent voyage
back to where
their day began.
the familiar tree
and branch and leaf.
where they will sleep,
where they are home –

fixers

we're wired with strong coffee
        and good intentions.

another day, another demo, we're
        going to fix things.

solidarity.

fight the powers that be.

we're going to fix
        broken people,

who are lined up along the street,
        hunched, and wrinkled,
        and a little smelly.

we're the entertainment today.

we're fit, we talk and plan,
        we eat the right foods,

we march to an inner beat.

the broken people lean back,
        fumble for another bottle,
        they're numb,
        their dark, deep eyes
        will not be fixed.

nonetheless.

like the lines of this poem,
        condensing chaos
        into order,

we'll keep trying.

tomorrow morning, in the park,

urban creatures – robert martens

we'll share our strong coffee
and good intentions
with broken people.

pale rider

midsummer, but
winter blows through our bones.
one came riding,
riding,
the herald of ice and snow,
lie down, cover your heads,
children,

judgment is coming –

for transgressions unnoticed,
for the plunder of boredom,
for the diversions of infertility.

the old man smiles,
apocalypse, he says gently,
is born
with every child.

midsummer, and
a hooded giant
gallops through our fears,
the north wind
where his face should be.

apocalypse came and went,
a gap in history.

urban creatures – robert martens

sunday morning in the suburbs

urban creatures – robert martens

sunday morning

1.

dreams are angel wings,
and the comfort is too much
to bear, the erotic cherubs,
that is, the charming nude
babes that plunge up and down
the naves of baroque churches,
no church for him, though,
or for anyone, the institution
draining to extinction like
the oil of dinosaur bones.

but enough.

from indolent, near orgasmic,
underground he will rise,
a new resurrection for a new
age, well, the sun is bright,
a slight breeze pleasures
the morning, he will
rise to be himself, and if
he has family, which he does,
that will be attended to, and then
perhaps coffee, or the lawn
may need trimming, or he may
wander down barking suburb
streets, or drive, randomly,
to a mall, there necessarily
is, always, world without end,
a purchase and a credit card.

2.

barbarians bore the burden
of wisdom black and white.

their hearts beat red and raw,
their bones sightless and sore.

our world does not alliterate,
he thinks, nor does it rhyme.

the rainbow-dazzled road,
the beep of buy and soul.

he yawns, inhales the colours
of our kinky comfort zone,

where black and white archaic,
and nothing, nothing to choose.

3.

barbarians they were
not, bellows the
screen evangelist,
no! our
forefathers knew
freedom, they
believed they would
choose
when that day comes

freedom, a raggy busker
sings, freedom,
i don't
have a home
but man
i'm free

and he, our heroic he,
reaches into his
wallet for a coin, the
government, he thinks,
really
should do something

4.

he must be giddy
from his three coffees
and four martinis,
and barely out of bed,
giddy by god, as the
busker morphs
into a free concert, a
concert for the free, he
swimming into the roar
of the crowd, all of them
proudly free and
they're gonna let ya
know it, in that
sucking screen vortex, where
all of us images,
free to do
free to go
as we please, our bills
paid by the suits
in blue, entertainment
as social enterprise – and then –

the noise falters,
there's a pounding
in his head, he
suffers the hunger
that won't let go,
well, the suits can
take care of it,
that's their mandate,
maybe another martini
to settle his brain

5.

shall i pity this one?

his investments are solid.

he lives in a land of human rights.

he enjoys his work.

and this is sunday,
a space he may officially
fill at random.

he's a good citizen,
votes the right way,
tax credits for the poor.

he doesn't complain,
rises weekdays at the assigned hour,
but on sundays...

sundays, boundless sundays...

you have a phone, little lamb,
whom will you call?

whose voice would you
dearly love to hear?

they're moving away,
leaving you alone
and utterly free.

shall i join him for a drink,
out of pity?

6.

he is so very spiritual
all things bright and beautiful
the good world in his heart

the earth is kind and bountiful
her voice always amenable
invites us to take part

in the great inimitable
mystery that is the
brand new age universe.

in childhood he was
confined within
four archaic religious walls,

were they controlling?
were they mere
children imposing

upon children? and
somewhere, far beyond
the confines of the city,

he's driving, flying,
birds twitter, rivers burble,
gods polka,

our universe of spiritual,
and altogether bountiful,
she rests within his heart –

wait a minute, says
the homeless man, hey
got a minute?

7.

and time has flown by
on the wings
of a snow white dove,
what time is it, what
day is it, perhaps
he should exert more discipline,
should he
make that call, should he
make that purchase, is today
a good time to invest,
after all there's nothing
else to do – except
omg his family, he'd
nearly forgotten, he's been
dreaming on angel wings –
and his kids howl with delight, his
wife grins and snuggles closer,
as they fly
on the giant digital snowbird ride
at the monster stupendous otherworldly
funpark, sugar and shrieks and shreds,
not quite spiritual
but close enough –

come monday he'll commute
down the freeway, park
in his spot, settle his mind
into the company database,
and he'll dream
of cherub wings,
of week's end,
of perfect peace,
of sunday forever sunday.

urban creatures – robert martens

urban creatures – robert martens

citylab whitecoats

urban creatures – robert martens

playing dice with the universe

Quantum entanglement is the phenomenon that occurs when a group of particles are generated, interact, or share spatial proximity in a way such that the quantum state of each particle of the group cannot be described independently of the state of the others, including when the particles are separated by a large distance. The topic of quantum entanglement is at the heart of the disparity between classical and quantum physics: entanglement is a primary feature of quantum mechanics not present in classical mechanics.

impossible existence. we
should not be here, or
over there. god does not play
dice with the universe, said
einstein, but yes he does,
as he tosses a chuckle
into the vast wastebin. this
particle is describable only
with metaphor. this particle
is entangled with that
particle, though separated
by a distance describable
only in poetry. science

is inadequate. the words
of our greatest lunacy
might suffice. he turned
with words of contempt. i
shuddered, held my silence,
wondered why. while on

the other side of the
planet, he turned with words
of friendship. i didn't
wonder why. we were

entangled in quantum
speech. in the impossible.

urban creatures – robert martens

Quantum mechanics differs from classical physics in that energy, momentum, angular momentum, and other quantities of a bound system are restricted to discrete values (quantization); objects have characteristics of both particles and waves (wave–particle duality); and there are limits to how accurately the value of a physical quantity can be predicted prior to its measurement, given a complete set of initial conditions (the uncertainty principle).

retreating inwards, he encounters
the unimaginable. the era
has changed. he can't abide
the revolution in his soul.
he talks, he smokes, he talks
of better times, he's immersed
inwards, he's fled with
refugees to the unimaginable.

and you shall be well,
i tell him. the quantum
of our souls, spinning,
electrons, protons, neutrons,
and further down, where
quarks can be named only
as music. as prayer. as
blessing. an infinite space

within, we're particles,
glued together by a force
that might love us. the kingdom

of heaven is within you.
among you. the sizzle
of nucleus touching nucleus,
of finger on finger. this power,

he says, of mutual song.

The expansion of the universe is the increase in distance between any two given gravitationally unbound parts of the observable universe with time. It is an intrinsic expansion whereby the scale of space itself changes. The universe does not expand "into" anything and does not require space to exist "outside" it.

each day she drives the expanding
universe. each day, the freeway
to work, to school, and her stress is
beyond the speed of light, there,
always just beyond. she's

arrived from a strange land, to
a strange land, and nothing
can be explained. travel
is faster by the day. there's
no conclusion, it curves back
upon itself, no edge, no
elsewhere. and the rage

i find on the freeway, she
says, my anxiety as i grip
the wheel, on and on and
nowhere. let's ride

together, i say, we'll
fall in love, alter
space and time, accelerate
into the mystery.

there will be (no) blood

what if, said the man with silicon lips,
this universe is
a simulation, and you
and i digits
in a system
of expanding code,
so what's the
point, friends,
moving from one
to zero

what if, said the creator with a finger on the phone,
your silicon lips
are made for
talking and
walking and
removing the nukes
from the silo
where the kids
might find them

what if, said the woman with bones and blood,
and there's no
way to end this
poem, but
come on in anyway,
rest your weary
neurons, i've
programmed wine
and bread into
the next reboot

space

and filling our empty spaces,
we know we have achieved
the fleshing of our lives

the vacancy of dawn,
the data of the day,
the business of every hour

i cannot let it rest,
it haunts my deepest dreams,
it has a selling price

fear, that decrepit ghost,
waits in reckless moments,
its voice that doesn't exist

we've filled it with dark matter,
our empty universe,
living abhors a vacuum

my dear friend, nothing matters,
and time and blood and mercy
keep spilling through empty spaces

$e=mc^2$

crisis is pounding at the door.
einstein ignores the commotion, he's
scratching out a new equation
that may fit the time.
albert, i say, with some annoyance,
is there nothing we can do?

einstein looks up.
he's irritated, too many
interruptions, he will not
answer the door.
my friend, he says,
setting down his pencil,
solutions are relatively few.

our lab is rocking and rolling.
it curves into future past,
riding at lightspeed
through the gravity of global crisis.
they're idiots, says einstein,
with their credos of straight lines.

albert, i say,
*i'm going for a stroll
to monitor the situation.*
fine, i will join you, says einstein,
and we walk together
into the recalculated universe.
crisis doesn't notice us,
keeps pounding as the door
melts backwards into a big bang.

ctrl-alt-delete

the tech corp ceo
and his sidekick nerd
stand on a stage
wide as the nation

we are living
they announce to the media
in a grand simulation
you are a generated image

you are an algorithm
they say with a smile
programmed by space
at the beginning of time

wild applause
but in the back row
a grumpy old man
leans back and yawns

the tech corp ceo
and his sidekick nerd
delete us one by one
with a smile

i'm basking
in the trash file
where it's dark and warm
where the deleted snooze

the grumpy old man
taps the restore key
we wake up
in the grouchy back row

where greetings and hugs
temper and kiss
the stage is empty
they've been deleted

urban creatures – robert martens

red lights and cellphone streets

urban creatures – robert martens

diagnosis

crazy world, he said over his
second, and sniggered, and glasses
clinked, *yeah* she said, *we're all
nuts*, and they ambled over to the
bar for another, while in that

city night traffic coughed and
crept, fortunes were gambled
and lost, and some sat with
coffee on balconies, overlooking
the sanctioned chaos below,

on shoppers, and wanderers, and
people of the street, and he tossed
his bottle in the dumpster, heard
in his unsettled mind the war of
all things, endless, unredeemable,

oh god, he prayed, *they're fucking crazy*.

it came upon a midnight clear

the ice storm cracked open our valley,
power was out for days, driving us one degree
east of normal.

nothing like darkness to singe the outer
soul, send our brainwaves reeling
to the nearest star.

the christmas legend was sung,
occupying soldiers, psychotic king,
child refugee.

since that lightsmitten birth,
two thousand years of wrong, darkness
rolling across the planet.

and now i gift you this absurd metaphor, our
houses, chilly and dark, we're waiting
for the return of light.

when the outage ended, we watched
refugees on the news network, sat
down to a hot breakfast.

call me when you have time

some lives are on hold.

some lives never change,
they have no beginning
or end.

they are the neighbours
we don't meet.

some lives smile timidly,
look away, stand
in a corner with a drink.

they are the friends
we vaguely remember.

> when the minister of goodwill
> travels through town,
> shakes hands,
> distributes leaflets that say
> *if you work hard*
> *if you believe*
> *this is the law*

some lives aren't lives
at all, according
to the law.

they are the faces we glimpse
in discarded photographs.

they are the keepers
of secrets,
unbroken code.

prayer #8 (after jeff tweedy)

breathe out your nothing
into the evolving
morning
your dreams will pop and
reappear
at the edge
of the universe
heat wave
fatigue in the arteries
the heckling of crows
earth leans over
to look at you
breathe out
swing low your legs
over the aching bed
energy does not equal
mass and
gravity curves only
through your bones
einstein was wrong
when he lost
his socks
in evolving paradise

prayer #7 (after jeff tweedy)

the bass player
never gets the girl
buried alive
in the middle of the band
driving it forward
pushing the beat
so here i stand
wanting a drink
and the stage
is old and ratty
and i'm playing deep
where no one goes
and she cries
and she lies
to the beat in my bones
as i stand before god
whatever you do
don't
feel sorry for me

prayer #6 (after jeff tweedy)

wait for it
the penny
the shoe
to drop
no he
won't wait won't wait
sees eternity before
and behind so he
floods the basement
with whisky and
dips his brain
in the golden sludge
and he rises
slowly
from the foundation
into dreamy
space where vampires
and angels make
incendiary love and he
rises
smoothly
to mars
on a wing and a prayer
where shakespeare is
waiting
to be or
not on the
rock red planet

prayer #5 (after jeff tweedy)

light a candle
curse the darkness
let's meet
in the middle
at the shadow lines
bisecting our nation
light a candle
for the addict
returning
to an empty house
to an empty glass
chaos and community
and all the crazy
betweens
shadow lines
i may choose
to live there
where the fissure runs
let's drink to that
let's light a candle
to my zigzag life

prayer #1 (after jeff tweedy)

mahalia jackson's singing
peace in the valley
she's in a church
between my ears
he's walking the dog
he lives between mountain peaks
rattled by rain
umbrellas and splash traffic
who wrote that tune
hello no
he's angry
averts his eyes oh
the anxiety of our generation
trapped in the suburbs
down in the valley
shall i ask mahalia
she's not listening
she's wailing the
saintly blues
can you hear her
hello my friend
he's not listening
her valley voice
of terror and praise

prayer #2 (after jeff tweedy)

the giant screen
in the pub
is flogging wrestling
a crowdish roar as magnificent
as the war
dragging on
overseas
where it belongs
spring is slow
showers and muddy sewers
we all have our demons,
she says
bites into her croissant
the streets are hard
as a warrior's dick
umbrellas and boots
and the first cherry blossoms
throw pink curses
at the night front
boys looking for a fight
girls looking down
at their phones down
ok we've lost it
but there's no war here
except on giant screens

pickup truckers hauling ass

when truckers die, there is silence
in heaven. when truckers wake up
before sunrise, all hell resides
in the fumes of their diesel. breakfast
is coffee and six strips of bacon.
when truckers hit the road, they believe
in the epic nature of their four by
fours, they drive where they want,
when they want. the rest of us
are consigned to purgatory. truckers
pound the pedal. truckers paint,
insulate, wire, hammer. they do
the essential things. after which, they
rise and say a word of blessing and
haul ass, there's work to do, their friends
are other truckers, their wives
are a beloved afterthought. when
truckers are done for the day, all
roads lead home. when truckers
lie down to the gratitude of
warm beds, there is silence in heaven.

and my cellphone kept talking

these streets are not for
walking, said the banker
to the thief, as they
crossed the dotted line,
stumbling over beer bottles
and exhaust pipes, and

the highway howled
like a ferrari in
heat, and they clenched
their briefcases, straightened
their ties, polished
their shoes, dodged

the decoded faces behind
steering wheels, because
the traffic lights had
expired, and the crosswalks
all led to underground
carparks, and then,

walk hard, said the
thief, keep close, my
banker brother, this
is the revolution, take
my hand, and they
walked into the blue

swirling through the towers,
walked up and over,
beyond the hurricane
of smashed cellphones
and crooked elevators, they
were made for walking

elegy for a pop star

the creak of ancient bones,
the blank of future time,
she dared to be mediocre.

her voice was lost in the stars,
the terror of world without end,
she sang with the softness of jello.

war and oppression and hunger,
a cosmos devoid of compassion,
she saved our souls with average.

so jeer at her middling talent,
smirk at her teenie tunes,
but her hits won't leave our brains.

tomorrow she'll be forgotten,
gone to delinquent night,
she felt that fear, and more,

but she dared to be mediocre.

urban creatures

urban creatures – robert martens

urban creatures

1.

i've always loved crows,
their raucous appetite,
their thieving voices. how
can you, i'm asked,
they're an ugly nuisance,
but that's precisely
what seduces me
into their world.

when morning comes,
their blackness emerges,
my nightstricken dreams
vanish. i'm nudged unwillingly
into day. the planet
is dying. winter is
coming. at the second
daily hour, i'm lifted,
black wings rising
in rivers of light.

2.

at dusk they come stalking,
seeing. those mystic
raccoon eyes. watch your
pets, i'm told, they are
predators, with those steel claws
they'll take what they can get.

at dusk she comes to my window.
her great round planetary eyes.
she peers, looks
past me to a world
unseen. forgotten. then
goes stalking, seeing
the spirits in my backyard.

3.

bong, they cry, bong you.
they fly in a ragged v.
canada geese are a tale of
success. they've proliferated
beyond what we like, we
addle their eggs to no avail,
canada goose babies appear
like a miracle. we ogle them,
feed them leftover crumbs.

ingrates. no thank yous.
a party of geese, feeding,
bonging. no regrets. they're
leaving for a warmer place,
the world will be brighter,
luckier, happier, just wait...
and when they return, all
will be gosling, all will be well.

4.

playing possum? is that
a myth? i've never seen it,
except in humans, pretending
to doze, feigning ignorance,
i do that every day. but

is this one playing possum?
this homely creature, buggy
eyes, protruding teeth, and
its guts spilling roadside.
i shall beat the drum slowly.
martyrs to our time, they
perish on altars of asphalt.
we might grimace and swerve,
steer round the hairy corpse.
another day, another victim.

5.

we kids watched them nest
in our holly tree. the little ones
raising their beaks to the mother,
to the morning sun. proudly, we
showed them to our friends. robin
redbreast. common robin. in
reality a thrush, but always
robin, wet with morning dew,
red flash of a spring day.

not so common robin now, their
nesting spaces bulldozed,
but they persist. the hop,
the lawn, the worm. we're
kids again, always, and
when we leave the nest, oh
that flight to the highest branch,
and all the world to see.

6.

they're tricksters. they're outlaws.
they don't belong. i once saw
a coyote as silver as desert
sand. they trot on the wind. they
leap canyons. they'll take
your cat or dog and laugh
about it the next day.

coyotes have gathered at
the edges, an invasion
is imminent, one at a time
they cross over, they erase
boundaries, they love the
chaos of their lonely bones.
stare at them long enough,
and you're an outlaw too.

7.

here. no, there. or then. maybe
now. time to dash. good morning,
good night. scamper. sprint
across the road. tail up.
always up. ready to go. go.
go. what was it then? or
now? anyway, got to go.

can't decide. squirrels. bushy
leap, stop, chew, run now
for your life. then, frozen
in time, a second of eternity,
pause, nibble, stare. perhaps
now. only now. tail up. we
will feed their cuteness.

8.

they rain on the just
and the unjust. they
shall not be moved.
this is their home.
they deposit white residue
on the good and the bad,
on the baby buggy, on
the statue of a madman.

we have gathered together,
sing the pigeons, and they
coo, and crap, and eat, and
coo. i cover my head
as i walk by. as they
wheel off in flight, together,
and settle down again on
branch and powerline and roof,
muttering gently all at once,
their church of crap and coo.

9.

they are loners by necessity.
the fragrance. the stink.
advisory: if you see the
white stripe down the back,
avoid, retreat, flee to your
comfortable abode. even
their name has evolved
into an insult – you skunk.
and so they walk alone.

i once encountered a pet
skunk, it was graceful,
petite, affectionate, it had been
deskunked. this was
by necessity. but to rob
this homeless creature of
its being. thus this prophecy:
one day they will be loved,
the stink will transform to
miraculous perfume, they will be
forgiven, and we comfortable,
we self-absorbed, all
creatures will be loved.

10.

our city has a thick skin.
impenetrable. a defence
against eternity. nothing here
shall pass. and wild things
survive, fly the clotted air,
creep through the concrete
night. denizens
of the urban zoo. at

midnight, when our defences
are down, they talk to us,
come home, come home.
refugees who have never
left. their chirps and growls
and yelps, graffiti
on the shells of our souls.

thick-skinned. when
we are gone, will they
dig at the rubble,
will they notice
our absence?

urban legends

urban creatures – robert martens

based on a true story

once again, i was being propositioned.
it had happened before, children of god
cult, amsterdam, and sex was the lure.
the girls were always gorgeous. helpful.
she would be good, if you would join god.

portland, oregon, a few years later,
three of us drinking our way through
downtown, sowing our wild oats, to
quote a previous farming generation,
and there she was, gorgeous, helpful,
was she children of god? she didn't
say, she was temptation, the bait
on the line of the master, and we three,
we didn't care, late night, ready for
sleep, but she'd invited us upstairs,
and who could say no, especially
when alcohol blurred the city air.

we followed her. the group was
waiting for us. what happened to the
girl? memory's dim and the years are
harsh, but we were set up one on one with
young guys, they were new to this fishing game,
we were not, we three had survived
years of proselytizing from people
with heavenly intentions, we knew the
rules, when the deck was shuffled
no one would win, and they gave us
pamphlets, this is the way, they said,
the only way, and one of us sat
with a fixed grin on a straight-backed
chair, he was a drunken fortress,
while i quoted tolstoy and kierkegaard
to the blank of my inquisitor's eyes, but

the third of us, in magnificent isolation,
ripped the pamphlets to shreds and
tossed them over his shoulder, i'll be forever

in his debt, the shower of paper,
the slight smile on his forgiving face.

white nights

after three days, i was saturated
with the boredom of it all. reno.
the one-armed bandits, catatonic
gamblers, the clink and chink of coin,
the booze, the bad jokes, and terminally
unfunny comedians, the entertainment
that could be endured only through
a drunken haze, the scant-clad
girls slinging drinks, the buzz
of inane conversation, the wins,
far more the losses, the lights, the
perpetual lights turning the night white,
and the gamblers white too, spending their
savings on things they wouldn't remember.

alone, i paced my way through
sudden darkness back to my econo
motel. i could hear the faint
thump thump at my back. i had turned to
flee the clamour. so i thought. at the
crosswalk, i hesitated. stopped.
a car making errant moves.
young black guys crowded inside.
windows open. *hey whitey's afraid
we're gonna run 'em down*. titters,
blasts of laughter. i stared straight ahead.
they drove on.

the white nights of reno. i had
carried them with me. i was
whitey incarnate, i was pink,
really, but there's no racial slur
for pink. i was the tourist they
envied, the rich dude they hated
with all their hearts. i wonder
if they've survived. if they have
gone on to better. if there are
crosswalks where whitey won't
grab them by the balls.

missing

1. the meds tuned his mind,
turned him passive
as a stone, so he
tossed them
into a cobwebbed corner
of his kitchen cabinet,
and in celebration
lobbed his furniture
out the patio door.

2. he wrote lines of poetry
that scribbled
a pathway between him
and the rest of us,
i was in nicaragua,
he said, when
the cia found me
wired to the waves.

3. i bought his coffee,
mended the conversation
as it squiggled
across the table,
gave him a dollar
or two, my rich
relatives, he said,
refuse to
look me in the eye.

4. he was a swaying
giant, lumbered
the streets into a
prehistoric past, drew
a knife, when he
emerged from prison,
he was fed and
dressed, and his
tongue worked.

5. don't give him
money, said the
psych nurse, did she
know something, was
compassion an archaic
thing, and the last time
he called me,
sorry no more money,
i said, look
what's happened –

6. you're the same as
the fuckin rest of 'em,
he said, and a
click, and a vanishing act,
he went up north,
or he stayed
in his room,
an absence,
a goodness
that smiles through
our daily disease.

unprotected borders
for a friend who no longer knows me

the boundaries of my lives
are sagging tonight,
touched with grey
and raggedly forgetful.
my lives, within this incoherence,
may encroach upon yours.
forgive the disruption.
the disorder is unintended,
emerging from a stellar explosion
at time's beginning.

yesterday she moved her boundaries,
hauled them back, slowly,
into erasure.
she asked who i was.
her wheelchair rolled her down the hallway
to former lives
that no longer existed.
if i can find her room,
we may collide in the confusion
at time's end.

shoeshine

on the carnival streets
of nairobi, pushes and shouts
and grit and the poverty
that wants to talk, that
won't leave you alone,
i had my sneakers
shined, yes, in nairobi
sneakers were shined,
scrubbed with a clear
liquid perhaps toxic,
i feared for the
lungs of the shiner,
and he brushed, and
towelled, wordlessly,
i've never been easy
with shoeshines, the
indignity of it, and a
local came by, dirty
and dead drunk, and he was
not a local, *i'm from
south africa sir*, he said,
*how are you sir, i
need fifty shillings for
the train, can you
give me sir*, and he
smiled, and talked, and
talked, fifteen minutes
of talk, *sir in my
country a white man
does not talk to me*,
and i cringed, but i
gave him the fifty, i
smiled, i was the
righteous white man,
i was not easy
with the indignity

cruising to byzantium

And therefore I have sailed the seas and come
To the holy city of Byzantium. (Yeats)

1.

a fuzzy start
      to a tale about nothing.

a long day. a vacuous day,
      and now an evening whisky,
      and memories swirling to zero.

breakfast. coffee. a stroll.
      pulling out of port, departing
      the continent. a
      twinge of regret.

lunch. (*something in between.*) dinner. entertainment. laughter.
      my brain profoundly fuzzed.

we're happy.

what happened?

2.

the open ocean.

the heave and swell,
      and years counting down.

my ancestral heritage tells me
      i should be doing something,
      that my life needs to be filled up
      like a festive balloon.

anxieties are rife here, but
      the fees have been paid, and
      worries are ejected with the compost.

so: no schedule.

: no tasks.

: no responsibilities.

sitting here, writing these words,
      may be a sea surge
      in the wrong direction.

3.

the cruise director is doing
        a happy dance.

the kind of skip hopping in the sky
        that you see in dreams.

is everyone fine?

applause. everyone's fine.

in this quasidream, this
        floating home, where troubles
        disappear with dessert.

where tomorrow is dozing.

an intrusion. a lecture
        by an environmentalist.
        what is she doing here?
        she talks about our polluted oceans.
        what is she doing here?

a break in the cumulus.
        a bluesilver sunspot on the sea.

each moment, says the zimbabwean server,
        is the best.

sail on, to
        byzantium and beyond.

4.

a week has gone.

vanished into the bubbling blue.

i try to focus. the thump of pop
       drifting on deck,
       through the pools, and
       into our beds. listen
       to *this* word only.
       this note.

have a good day ... more coffee sir? ...
       would you like a drink? ...
       nice to see you again ... can you
       focus on this moment?

time is crowd chatter and lounge bands.

time is an empty glass.

time is the final set,
       the last dance,
       luv ya,
       see ya tomorrow.

5.

an unceasing drizzle today,
a grey japanese port,
and a friend has died.

off the ship, a giant
buddha, a temple, a man
with a bamboo flute.

two women playing the koto,
playing the new moon,
and amazing grace.

sacred space, remove
your shoes, the buddha
beyond grief and joy.

back on the ship, a
new presence, and
nothing has changed,

yet, this transfiguration,
this sea of sorrow, of
happiness, this sacred space.

call now! retire in the city!

urban creatures – robert martens

the mystery of our aging

1.

upon these knotted hands,
this tongue,
this diminishment of words –

upon this wounded earth,
this soil, our
troubled winds and streams –

a light from the opposite universe,
from the deepest funnel of spacetime,
has come for us,
for the mystery of our aging,
to touch us, gently,
each of our lives
examined, dropped, forgotten.

but the cruelty of light,

so hard on weak eyes,

and i want to sleep

2.

a time there was,
or passing time,
when we white knuckled
down the freeway,

from point a to b,
alpha to omega,
and irrelevance between,
a time there was,

or no time at all,
but distance now
too stretched for old bones,
foot off the pedal,

as the freeway recedes
into cosmic infinity,
gear down, my friend,
as we arrive,

time billowing behind,
or time forgotten,
through space measured
by ancient hands

3.

language is a stutter.

a flutter,
like a bird, i forget words,
she says, but i'm assured
it's not dementia.

silence expands,
folds over itself.

infinite spaces
between words,

the vacuum.

nature abhors a vacuum,
or so we are told,
the slow, sure slide
unobservable, of
mountain into valley,
and you are there,

as we are emptied,
as the earth flattens,

as you receive me,
my enemy, my friend.

come for a visit, she says,
we'll talk in fragments

4.

Pray, do not mock me:
I am a very foolish fond old man,
Fourscore and upward, not an hour more or less;
And, to deal plainly,
I fear I am not in my perfect mind. – King Lear

am i speaking in abstractions?

my apologies. i'll tell
      the story of wrinkles and warts,
      of creaking bones and thinning blood,
      of stumbles
      on the stairway to heaven.

yesterday, the years gathered at our table, and
      we joked about our infirmities.

can you drink your morning coffee
      without slurping? without

pursing your shrunken lips?

do not mock me. i am a foolish old man.

and though my hearing is leaving,
      fading to some impenetrable centre,

still, i can listen.

when the five senses go dead,
      one by one,

your voice is clear as a star
      over bethlehem.

5.

fear of falling.

freefall.

spring summer fall,

jokes on aging,
the old in their airless homes,
tangled by
an invisible line
that snags and trips them
into vacancy.

an old frail heart
plummets. and

as we fall with alice
down the rabbit hole,
wonderland awaits,

the earth is falling,
you and i holding each other, because

the young fall too,

but we the old,
the smile of the cheshire cat,
such a dream it was,
our beautiful dreamer

6.

i'll write these words
before i slide
into anonymity.

my eyes wide open
at the table
of the empty cup.

nothing matters, says
the cynic, and nothing matters
for the lover.

morning is coming,
table and cup,
visit me when words are gone,

when the sun rises
on the invisible man,
and all the billions,

anonymous from birth,
tossed from earth's cradle,
and i just one,

waiting for the nostalgic melody
at the end of time,
bless me now, i have sinned

7.

grumpy old men.
(and women)
it's true.

their noses sharpen,
their chins twist accusingly,
their cheeks furrow
into scowls
that pin down the brain,
and they invariably stand
in my way.

their sins clarify with age,
they cut me off at the intersection,
they refuse to look me in the eye,
they dwell in paranoia.

do i love them? yes,

because i'm grumpy too,

because

when i straighten my shoulders,

and lift my eyes unto the hills,

and they forgive me,
if only for a moment,

old saints?

it's true.

8.

and this must end

may flights of angels sing thee

and this will end

what does it matter

your x, my y

our gentled bones

our eyes peering inwards

to our regrets

that never were, and shall not be

your a, my b

our wrinkled brows

our hair dusted by time

by love

that never was, and shall be

always

held between us

precariously

in the ache of our fingers

comedy club, cash bar only

urban creatures – robert martens

can one, let me see, how do i phrase this, can one judge without anger?

i'm surrounded, she says,
by poets
who write for other poets,
her chin's upright,
her shoulders pinned back
like the people's judge. and

i don't want to be
angry, but
this morning,
having read a poet
who writes for other poets,
his postmodern-awarded-nothing-really-matters-scribble –

there's a hard november rain,
a slant in the west wind,
this may be
his day of judgment –

and as my neighbour
drives his truck off to work,
we wave,
acknowledge the wet and cold,
the weather that really matters – as

i the people's judge

toss the poems he wrote for other poets

ceremonially –

poetically –

without anger –

into the dumpster.

not the minutes

the committee for the mennonite periodical
        has convened.

i write the minutes.

the minutes, i am thinking,
        will vanish into the infinite void of time.

mennonites, as you can see, can
        find the dark lining on any silver cloud.

our coffee cups are half empty.
        in other words, not half full.

but we chatter on,
as mennonites do,

they remain social creatures, even after
        their communities have vanished.

we discuss all those concerns
        irrelevant to the periodical,
        a lunatic president, social isolation,
        pandemics, pervasive corruption.

we talk about the global web of lies
        that on any given morning
        is stickier than the morning before.

ach, says louise, i've become
        too old for this world.

that, i say,
        should be in the minutes.

it is not.

it is here,
        in the dubious lines of this poem.

the drunkard's farewell

his thesis is correct. living
        is intolerable. the world
        is an enormous butcher knife.

or cross, to speak in theological terms.

he has drunk his last drink. he has
        chewed his final burger.

the time has come to bid farewell
        to his long, wretched existence,
        to his road metaphorically and literally
        strewn with empty bottles.

the angel of death takes his hand.

the drunkard is pleasantly surprised.
        death isn't so bad. the
        angel of death leads him
        to a corner table, where
        a colossal bottle of red wine
        awaits his approval.

the pub of death is bright and warm.
        conversation is high decibel,
        millions of addicts, their
        suffering over, chortling and shrieking,
        expostulating, their breath
        rising in a lucid white fog.

have another, says the angel of death.
        we have enough in stock
        for at least one eternity.

the drunkard wakes up. of course
        it was a dream, as clichéd
        as his life. as
        our lives.
i will live another day, he says, if i must.

just one more day, says the angel of death.
    here, have another.

the red dog barks at midnight

four of them, male
or female it's hard to
tell, they're so drunk
their faces are
a blur.

four of them on
the freedom trail,
waving flags, it's
our god-given right
to smirk.

four of them,
horsemen of the
petty apocalypse,
clichés fizzing from
their lips.

four of them
mugging for screens,
the poor oh yeah,
well, they can have
leftovers.

four of them
at the door,
at your table, they
need your love because they don't
deserve it.

four of them
needing medicine and
tender loving care, but
i'm done and this poem
is over.

buddha and the guys

but buddha, good buddy, you said that
    all existence is suffering.

yeah ...

he nods. petulantly. he has a headache.

and that all suffering can be transcended,
    i say.

well, yeah, but sometimes ...

he's enthroned in magnificence,
    flowing red-gold robes,
        pillows, wall tapestries, scattered lotus,
    and in the corner of his cave,

discarded empties. cigarette butts.

it's a bit overwhelming some days,
    he says, to be the leader
    of a global religion. sometimes,
    he says, we all need to
    escape.

the universal, knowing smile
    never leaves his lips.
    a spring breeze hovers
    blue-green
    at the cave entrance.

but, i say, nirvana ...
    perfection ...

buddha rubs his eyes.

and sighs.

the smile never leaves his lips.

nirvana, he says, can only
        take you so far, and then ...

... long pause ...

... and then you're on your own,
        even in nirvana.

footsteps outside the cave. muffled chatter.

there's my company, he says,
        a couple of guys
        who lead global religions,
        we're gonna have a few,
        and maybe some lady friends ...

the music of the sun
        flares at his fingertips.

... anyway, i'll see you tomorrow, he says,
        later in the day,
        morning will be busy,
        i have some transcending to do.

the community of saints

the booze group of the idle rednecks
        has convened.

i don't believe it, says A,
        and neither should you.

they're all assholes, says B,
        they wanna force us
        to believe it.

don't believe anything, says C.

the barkeep arrives with another round of beer.
        it foams and glows
        with transcendent light.

heads up, says A.

i don't believe it, says B,
        did you catch the wrestling last night?

no, says C, i was nuking
        a frozen pizza
        and forgot about it.

don't believe anything, says A.

touchdown! a! play! for! the! ages!
        shouts the sportscaster
        on eleven screens.

that should've been a penalty,
        says B, the referee's
        an asshole, someone
        paid him off.

the game's a scam
        says C.

urban creatures – robert martens

lights out, says the barkeep,
     it's past closing time,
        and you were never here.

a nostalgic look back

no regrets, you say, looking back in time
        you would change nothing. i say,

start with regrets. i say,

my life has been a series of bad decisions.

i added too much salt to the pasta.
        bad decision.

i adopted a cat that slobbered when he purred.
        ditto.

this is a poem of lists.

i moved the potted heather and it died.

i attacked a friend for his faults. which were
        bad decisions on his part, and a
        lack of perspective on mine.

i left her at the bar
        and never saw her again.

i declined a career i might have loved.
        or perhaps not.

i backed away from a potential friendship
        on a chilly damp morning.

i overthrew the government and the fascists won.

i poisoned the earth.

i waged war on imagined enemies.

i sent the poor and dispossessed to prison.

urban creatures – robert martens

i dropped a nuclear bomb
    on those who deserved it.

some of the items on this list
    are not strictly true.

perhaps writing this poem
    was a bad decision.

i will add it to my regrets.

urban creatures – robert martens

urban creatures – robert martens

four-part harmony on golden streets

urban creatures – robert martens

pandemic in the suburbs

> *in these heavy times*, she said,
> *i can barely step out of bed.*

have you heard the sweatshop clamour?
the knock of hunger at the door?

in this land of wine and roses,
we've learned to ignore the borderlands.

come together, let's talk,
heavy times rise in the morning,

come together, let's kneel,
let's pray to the forgotten ones,

to their bright, forgiving god,
their crashing, empty skies.

> *i understand*, i said,
> *call me when you get up.*

then and now and then

the young man is startled.
or perhaps not. it's late,
and dark, and why
has he glanced up
to see the stars
pulling together? into
a single pulsating drop,
a tear? in that moment,
his life is clear. his
standing there.
the galaxies in his eyes.

which are receding now,
accelerating beyond
the speed of light,
to the edge of the universe.
or perhaps not.
the edge doesn't
exist. his aged heart
wants to travel with them,
with the galaxies
speeding away.
pulling together.

in every grain of sand

in every leaf and pebble
she hears the voices,
the questions of what
she once was but

on this day scorched
by the rays of
a quantum sun,
in our galaxy

far far away, beyond
all questions, and another
friend gone, the sadness
he kept on his skin,

a tattoo of a birth
gone wrong and a city
that took away his
breath, yet

every leaf and pebble,
their questions, their
quiet invitation to join
what we once were

resurrection between the lines

after the cruel months of snow,
rain and fog, they emerge,
they've persisted, somewhere,
somehow.

new nests, winged formations
across the sky, birdsong,
mating, and the damp earth
welcoming.

this miracle of universal return,
don't explain it,
let it be touched
by wonder.

he's built a cellular wall against it,
click and tweet of protection,
there's nothing for him
outside.   yet,

after the cruel months of birth,
of death, he emerges,
he's persisted through liquor
and platitudes.

flights of love around him,
he can't explain it,
and walls too, and
rainy nights.

noise data

her head was a video race
through the globe's gangster streets,
tenements tottered and phones crashed,
bills were paid with an involuntary
blink of the eye, and oh that
pop music with a beat so fixed
you could set your heart to it.

anxiety. it wasn't a fog, but
a thumping clamour from
tomorrow. she couldn't
stand outside it. locked in
tight as medusa's skull.

she was never alone. a pandemic,
a contagion, it spread like
dementia, we gunned through
waves of future sound, the vibrations
sucked out our brain cells
one by one, until war
was the conclusion, war
was the only logical
move, she was always
alone, as missiles were
bought and sold on the
planetary virus market.

and she laughed. was she
beyond redemption, was she
crazed? she walked, and
laughed, and prayed,
and no one knew prayer,
and she ... she walked.

coffee cantata

the first sip, a black and hearty
welcome. under normal conditions, that is.
today's a puzzle, the coffee
isn't itself, it tastes of
caverns littered with
dinosaur bones. this morning there's
no solution in her morning cup.

across town, he
downs his latte in
a money minute,
contemplates the
ruthless rush, the mad
meetings, the confabs
curdling on his tongue,
there's something faintly
sexual in a coffee
mug, and he thinks of
her, texts her
with three emojis.

justice, they agree, has drowned
in a river of stale coffee.

they shed a tear over lost things,
carry on the sexuality
of small talk.
tonight, she says,
the city will coalesce
into justice, into the purest,
blackest love. if you
say so, he says.

are you ready? she asks,
i've put on a fresh pot.

average

the average man
is a useful thing.
likewise the average woman.
they make the world go round
and arrive at the same place
the next day.

they utter a cliché
to mark the dawn.
the average cliché
finds new life in social media,
spawning new generations
of average speech.

the typical researcher
arrives at work daily,
anxious to propagate new data.
the resulting algorithms
indicate that someone dies
with every cliché.

as a typical and average poet,
who nonetheless is tainted
by miracle, i
dream that every kind word
rides a fresh wind
in the quantum of the average soul.

mistakes

mistakes will set you free.
the prayer tossed in the can.

the word dropped at the curb.
the smile, your unctuous smile.

god knows you aren't perfect.
your best friend told you so.

the jeer raised at the rally.
the irony in your belly.

perhaps your life is wasted.
the bible tells you so.

rain on a muddy pond.
the placid shapes of geese.

your neighbour leans to talk.
that gift left at your door.

mistakes will set you free.
the rhythms of your day.

the highs and lows

1.

more weary she could not be.
had left her country, those
she loved. new to everything.
even the dust is strange, a novel
quality of drift. and the hour
before, she'd sunk into her chair.

another grand world beneath thee.
mirrors under her toes,
where country and lovers sing
through dust to her fabled few.
the shock of towers above her.
and holy the time to those who care.

2.

he's lived here since birth,
but is not home. he,
and she, divided, divorced,
this day and days of banality.
they speak to each other across
time zones, she's discovered

a holy beneath her feet,
but he is lifted to the winds,
above this globe slashed
by sunfire, so suddenly
carried to the river, to her,
where dust and wind on their tongues.

winter solstice

1.

the weight of darkness,
falling from space,
from the immensity,
beyond, beyond,

onto this tiny globe,
its green and blue
dimmed to shadow,
our faces turned

from the sun,
from light, from
the lightness of being,
our stubborn refusal,

our war, eternal,
black lava
in our veins,
in earth's core,

when birth, resurrection,
the revolving spark,
our words of darkness,
our stubborn refusal,

turn again, and again,
green and blue
catching the planet
as it falls into light

2.

her half-shut eyes.

and myself, drowsing,
my half-state
of being. then,

startled awake by
crows flapping through
the bare bones
of maple.

keep walking, she says,
as her half-life
unfolds, the
shadows, the shadows
rippling above the lake. and

tomorrow
will rise brighter, but

this morning,
on the shortest day
of the year,
a grey sun
smouldering
on damp soil, in
my opening eyes.

anger

1.

something sinister hangs between us,
invisible, yet acid to the touch,
ours is a troubled era, proclaims
the news network, as though hatred
is something new, and yet

here it is again, that ancient
crackling in the soul, and
when i turn to her, turn to her,
her face is stone, unchangeable,
and so will ever be, and yet

we must go on. sometimes
love is at a loss, like yesterdays
counted and forgotten. still,
grace is in the step taken,
the repositioning of faith and flesh.

2.

yet something miraculous hovers
between us, the morning after,
the rush of words last night
that settled like mosquitoes
on the skin, and her face

fleetingly blank, remembering
the ice storm of abuse,
the dialectic of power inherited
from tedious yesterdays, the
anxieties grasping for control,

and yet she goes on. we're
forgiven, somehow. love,
after all, is real, steps
taken, words spoken, our
astonishing reservoir of good will.

3.

faith was sold at a discount
during the financial blight.

the geese knew nothing of it,
wheeled in flight, turned north.

a warm wind rippled over
the lake, and certainty – certainty –

all will be well, the planet's
turning engraved on our hearts.

and on our tongues. a moment later,
the usual. again. banality,

trivial quarrels. yet
it was wonderful, our days

measured by nothing in particular,
city traffic, screens, signatures,

a cup together, a word or two
between bursts of war and peace.

household spirit

*"Unseen protector of the peaceful manor,
O kindly spirit of the home." Aleksandr Pushkin*

unseen protector of
the peaceful manor, i
heard you shuffling
papers in the early
hours, will you
arrange us this
day, so that mornings
may begin again,
that this spray of
light might overtake
the farthest expanding
star, and the
homeless heart?

o kindly spirit
of the home, i
heard your tired
grumbling at midnight,
will you bequeath
grace on this time
that flows inexorably
through the dark, so that
ancestors might sit with
future ghosts, that
our hands may
touch theirs in
final thanksgiving?

sometimes

sometimes i think
what's the point, sometimes
our born brutality, our
love of violence,
of war, of abuse,
of indifference, does anyone
care, what's the point,
the few of us, the
rage against the machine,

what's the point, on
a globe where only
big counts, big
battles, big
politics, big
money, and

sometimes that's the
lie, there is, there
is a point, we can
step into the day,
small steady steps, we can
feed and clothe
the least of these,
we can love
minute by minute

Author Profile

Robert Martens grew up in a village of Russian Mennonite refugees, where trauma, mutual self-help, and a degree of community control were commonplace. During Simon Fraser University's "long-hair" years of student rebellion, he quickly absorbed the individualistic values of Western society. Robert lives in the city of Abbotsford, BC, where he has edited and written local histories, and published a series of books of poetry. He grieves our world's loss, or even denial, of the concepts of community and home.

www.ingramcontent.com/pod-product-compliance
Lightning Source LLC
Chambersburg PA
CBHW071246070526
44583CB00017B/2343